SHIRE NATURAL HI**

CW00959702

THE
GOLDEN EAGLE

JOHN LOVE
and JEFF WATSON

CONTENTS

Cover: *The head of an immature golden eagle.*

Series editor: Jim Flegg.

Copyright © 1990 by John Love and Jeff Watson. First published 1990.
Number 56 in the Shire Natural History series. ISBN 0 7478 0091 X.
All rights reserved. No part of this publication may be reproduced or transmitted in any
form or by any means, electronic or mechanical, including photocopy, recording, or any
information storage and retrieval system, without permission in writing from the publishers,
Shire Publications Ltd, Cromwell House, Church Street, Princes Risborough,
Buckinghamshire HP17 9AJ, UK.

British Library Cataloguing in Publication Data:
Love, John.
The Golden Eagle.
1. Golden Eagles — personal observations.
I. Title. II. Watson, Jeff.
598.916

Printed in Great Britain by C. I. Thomas & Sons (Haverfordwest) Ltd,
Press Buildings, Merlins Bridge, Haverfordwest, Dyfed, SA61 1XF.

Introduction and description

The golden eagle (*Aquila chrysaetos*) is considered to be the 'king of birds'. It is everything the popular imagination demands of an eagle. It is majestic in appearance, long-lived, hook-beaked, keen-eyed and a master of the skies. It is swift and successful as a predator and lives in remote but beautiful wild country.

Few people are lucky enough ever to see one, yet it is one of the most familiar of birds. From time immemorial it has figured in fable and folklore, falconry, heraldry, art and sculpture. It is the bird that visitors most hope to see when they venture north into the Highlands of Scotland. However, in the wild it is shy, retiring and inhabits rugged mountainous regions far removed from the haunts of man.

In falconry golden eagles were the sole preserve of kings and emperors, with hawks and falcons being flown by lesser mortals. Nowadays few people have the time, the patience or the legal permits required to train eagles. In central Asia Kirghiz tribesmen long used golden eagles to kill gazelles, wild goats, foxes and even wolves.

The golden eagle's upperparts are a tawny brown colour fading somewhat on the wing coverts. The underside is dark brown, while the primary and secondary feathers on each wing are almost black. The tail feathers are paler with a suggestion of darker banding. It is the pale golden plumes on the head and back of the neck which give the bird its name. The eye is a chestnut brown and the bill a horny grey colour. The bare skin around the nostrils and edge of the face is pale yellow. The legs are feathered in light brown right down to the toes, a characteristic of the 'true or booted eagles', to which group the golden eagle belongs. The talons are bright yellow, tipped with the long black claws which are the tools of the eagle's predatory trade.

The juvenile is similar, although a somewhat darker and richer brown. Its neck plumes are more rufous than golden, sometimes streaked in white. But the most striking difference lies in the large white patches in the centre of each wing (top and bottom), and the conspicuous white base to the tail, which terminates in a broad black band. These features gradually darken as the bird assumes the adult dress, at an age of about five years. Moult is complicated and prolonged, it taking several summers for the bird to replace all its feathers.

The white on the wings and tail of a juvenile golden eagle is most obvious in flight and often tempts confusion with the white-tailed sea eagle (*Haliaeetus albicilla*). This is the only other British eagle and is being reintroduced to its old haunts (Love, 1983). However, the longer rectangular tail and short neck of the golden eagle are diagnostic. The golden eagle can reach 2.2 metres (7 feet 2 inches) in wingspan, a sea eagle 0.5 metre (1 foot 8 inches) more. In contrast a buzzard's is only about 1.5 metres (5 feet). A golden eagle can weigh up to 7 kg (15 pounds).

In common with many birds of prey, it is the male golden eagle which is the smaller of the sexes. In wing length the difference is about 10 to 12 per cent, in body weight nearly 30 per cent. This phenomenon is termed 'reversed sexual dimorphism' — reversed because in most other birds it is the female which is the smaller. Newton (1979) reviewed the various hypotheses to account for this reversal, relating it to feeding habits. There is hardly any size difference amongst the carrion-feeding vultures and condors, for instance, while the bird-catching sparrowhawk lies at the other extreme, with the female twice the size of the male. The golden eagle comes somewhere in between and does not offer much insight to the biologist seeking a solution to the conundrum. It is possible that the male is the size best suited to fulfil his role as a provider for both his mate and his family, catching smaller prey species which are also more abundant. This releases the female from hunting while she is carrying the eggs (reduc-

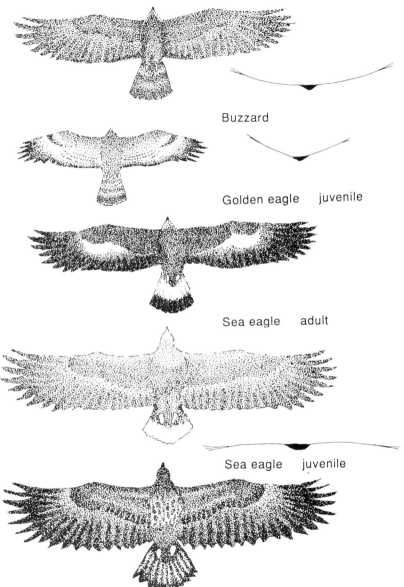

Golden eagle   adult

Buzzard

Golden eagle   juvenile

Sea eagle   adult

Sea eagle   juvenile

1. *Identification of British eagles. Buzzard plumage is very variable and usually more variegated than that of an eagle. The area of white on the wings and tail of the young golden eagle gradually diminishes as it matures to adulthood at five years or so.*

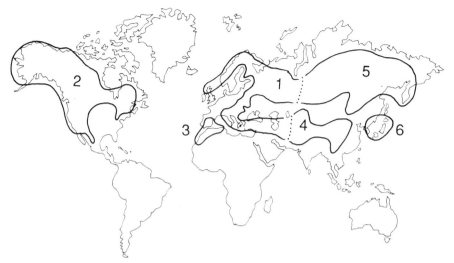

2. World distribution of the golden eagle and its subspecies: 1, Aquila chrysaetos chrysaetos; 2, A. c. canadensis; 3, A. c. homeyeri; 4, A. c. daphanea; 5, A. c. kamtschatika; 6, A. c. japonica.

ing the risk of damaging them) and during incubation and early brooding. When she is finally able to leave the growing young unattended, she can because of her larger size hunt larger prey and thus better contribute to the food supply. Being bigger than the male, she is also well equipped to defend the nest and young.

Golden eagles are relatively silent creatures and it is rare to hear them call much. When they do, during courtship and mating for instance, their terrier-like utterances are usually audible only at close quarters. Hungry youngsters in a nest can be more vociferous.

Distribution and persecution

The golden eagle has a cosmopolitan distribution, but in the northern hemisphere only. It ranges widely in North America. In Eurasia it occurs from the fringes of the Arctic to North Africa,

and from Britain in the west to Japan in the east. Across this vast tract of country are found six distinct races, each varying slightly in size and coloration. Those from Japan and North Africa tend to be the smallest, while Siberian eagles are the largest. The American form is the darkest, its neck plumes being more rufous than golden. Russian and Scandinavian birds are the palest representatives of the species. Scottish golden eagles are intermediate in coloration and are relatively large.

Within Britain the species is largely confined to Scotland. A few pairs occur in Galloway with the remainder being found north of the Highland line. Eagles range above the 700 metre (2300 foot) contour in the east but in the west Highlands they may nest near sea level. Some of these coastal eyries were formerly tenanted by white-tailed sea eagles before that species became extinct in Britain early in the twentieth century. First estimates of the Scottish golden eagle population in the 1950s and 1960s ranged from 150 to 300 breeding pairs. A more complete survey was undertaken in 1982/3 by the Royal Society for the Protection of Birds and the Nature Conservancy Council. This revealed a total of 424 breeding pairs, which represents

4

3. *Immature golden eagle taking flight and showing the white wing patches. Eagles' legs when dangling like this are seen to be very long.*

4. *Distribution of the golden eagle in Britain, from 'The Atlas of Breeding Birds in Britain and Ireland' (editor J. T. R. Sharrock), 1976.*

nearly 20 per cent of the entire European population (Dennis *et al*, 1984). These results do not necessarily reflect a recent increase in numbers, rather that the latest census was probably more efficient. Nevertheless it is true that the golden eagle has increased in the twentieth century, but by the First World War they had been at an all-time low.

Birds of prey, especially eagles, were persecuted relentlessly in the interests of game and livestock. By the eighteenth century in the north of England a bounty of 6d was paid for a young eagle, and a shilling for an adult. Between 1713 and 1765 over thirty eagles (probably both golden and sea) were killed in the Lakeland parish of Crosthwaite alone. Nests were also being robbed, 'it being a common species of traffic in this country to supply the curious with young eagles'.

Golden eagles ceased to breed in the Lake District in the first half of the nineteenth century, having already been wiped out in other upland districts of England and Wales. It was around this

time too that the Scottish eagles began to suffer, as sheep farming became a dominant land use in the Highlands and sporting estates began to flourish. In Sutherland and Caithness, for example, 10 shillings were being offered for the head and talons of a full grown eagle, 5 shillings for an eaglet and 2s 6d for every egg. Within the first six years of the 1820s nearly three hundred adults and sixty young or eggs were destroyed on one estate alone; a further 171 eagles and 53 young or eggs were taken between 1831 and 1834. These totals include both golden and sea eagles but do highlight the degree of animosity which prevailed. By this time egg collecting was becoming a fashionable pursuit and intensified the threat to the eagles. Golden eagle nests were located in remote and often inaccessible glens so eggs fetched high prices from Victorian collectors in the south. John Wolley was one who could boast over fifty Scottish golden eagle eggs in his cabinets. Another notorious egger lifted over one hundred eggs between 1870 and 1895. Egg collecting flourished until it was outlawed in 1954, but some die-hards persist in their nefarious habit even now.

By 1916 the white-tailed sea eagle had become extinct. Remarkably, however, the golden eagle was able to withstand all this pressure, if only in a handful of mountain retreats. The First World War, and later the Second, gave respite while men were engaged on the battlefields of Europe and elsewhere. This, together with eventual legal protection, enabled the species to stage a gradual recovery.

The golden eagle died out in Ireland and has never been able to return because poison baits are still used widely. One pair nested in County Antrim between 1953 and 1960 and apparently regularly commuted to the Scottish coast nearby in search of rabbits. Neither have golden eagles returned to Wales, so their legendary haunts on Snowdon (once known as *Creig ian'r Eryri*, the rock of eagles) remain vacant. One pair has settled in England, however, breeding in Lakeland every year since 1969 with considerable success, if only because rigorous wardening minimises human interference. This pair probably originated from

Galloway in south-west Scotland, where a few pairs made a comeback after 1945.

The 1982 golden eagle survey identified six hundred home ranges which probably once held breeding pairs. Most were checked in 1982, the remainder in 1983. About one-third were found unoccupied or else held only a single unpaired bird. Some of these localities are no longer suitable because of modern developments, but persecution is still a limiting factor, especially in the eastern Highlands.

Pat Sandeman (1957) first argued that the presence of lone golden eagles or of breeding immatures was indicative of persecution and was especially prevalent on grouse moors, which are the dominant land use in the eastern Highlands. The higher ground in the central Highlands is better suited to deer forest and stalkers are more tolerant of eagles. Indeed, Sandeman found that the eagles' breeding success in deer forest was twice that on grouse moor.

The 1982 survey confirmed that persecution still takes place. The percentage of unoccupied home ranges and the incidence of single birds on territories remain high in the eastern Highlands.

Diet and hunting techniques

Since golden eagles have a wide distribution in the northern hemisphere it is not surprising that they also have a very varied diet and a variety of hunting techniques. They have been seen on the ground, searching under stones for invertebrates or small reptiles, and will even drop tortoises from a height to crack open the shell. They have been watched feinting at a rattlesnake to make it uncoil before seizing it behind the head with the talons. Golden eagles may even wade into the shallows to snatch spent salmon from a river. Nor are they averse to piracy, stealing lumpsuckers or

pike from otters or gulls, or else trying to appropriate a fresh-killed hare from a wildcat. Nestling songbirds such as ring ouzels have been found in golden eagle eyries. The list of small or medium-sized birds and mammals featuring on the menu is vast — from larks to cranes, road-runners to wildfowl, and field mice to porcupines and deer. Marmots are important prey in the Alps and jack-rabbits in North America. In Scotland hares, rabbits and grouse are the favoured prey. Twelve rabbits were counted lying beside an eaglet in one Scottish eyrie, while at another it was estimated that 94 per cent of the prey were rabbits or hares (lagomorphs). One pair in the Hebrides appeared to specialise in feral cats, while on the mainland of Scotland fox cubs are not uncommonly taken. On the Hebridean island of Rum golden eagles regularly prey on brown rats and

5. *The relative proportions of different prey items in the diet of golden eagles in summer and in winter, in the west Highlands, the east Highlands and the Hebridean islands.*

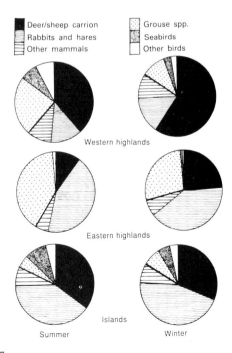

■ Deer/sheep carrion
▨ Rabbits and hares
▤ Other mammals

▨ Grouse spp.
▨ Seabirds
□ Other birds

Western highlands

Eastern highlands

Islands

Summer   Winter

6. *Typical golden eagle habitat in the east Highlands (Easter Ross); the dry heather moorland offers abundant prey in the form of mountain hares and grouse.*

7. *A golden eagle roost site, perhaps formerly a nesting site.*

8 (left). *Adult female golden eagle standing on its nest and showing the rich golden colour of its neck plumes to full advantage.*
9 (right). *An immature golden eagle eating a rabbit, those suffering from myxomatosis being particularly easy prey.*
10. *A juvenile golden eagle pouncing on small prey on the ground. Medium-sized animals such as rabbits, hares and grouse are more normal.*

seabirds, including Manx shearwaters, which are vulnerable as they come into their nest burrows at dusk. Any large mammals feature on the menu only as carrion, especially in the winter months when live prey may be scarce. Deer and sheep are commonly recorded in the Scottish Highlands, reindeer in northern Scandinavia, roe or chamois in the Alps, and wild boar and elk in the USSR.

A study of the diet of golden eagles (Watson *et al*, 1987) gives a picture of the food taken in different parts of Scotland and in different seasons. These data are derived from over three thousand prey items identified in pellets collected during 1982-5. Inevitably there is bias in any indirect measure of food such as this, and therefore the absolute figures should be treated with caution. However, the broad comparisons between areas and seasons are a fair assessment since the same methods were used throughout.

The overwhelming importance of carrion in winter is apparent for eagles from the west Highlands. In contrast lagomorphs and grouse dominate in the east Highlands (both summer and winter). In summer over 80 per cent of items identified here were just three species: red grouse, ptarmigan and mountain hare. The diet on the islands is intriguing for the remarkable consistency between summer and winter. This presumably reflects the mild oceanic climate of the Hebrides throughout the year.

The necessarily simplified representation of diet given in the figure inevitably disguises some interesting aspects of feeding ecology. For example, in the west Highlands the winter carrion component is principally deer in the north but sheep in the south (Argyll and Lochaber). The catholic nature of the summer diet in the west Highlands is hinted at by the relatively large proportion of 'other birds' and 'other mammals'. The list of these includes such species as fox, stoat, weasel, brown rat, water vole, hedgehog, hooded crow, short-eared owl, mistle thrush, mallard, heron and even kestrel, merlin and peregrine falcon. In the islands, at least in summer, the seabirds (principally fulmar) equal all other birds combined, and here also the rabbit is much more important than

the mountain hare, which dominates the lagomorph component on the mainland.

Many of the key differences in diet contribute to differences in the population dynamics of eagles across the range of Scotland, and we will return to this subject in the final chapter.

Most prey is first located as the eagle flies low over the hillside, quartering the ground methodically. More rarely an animal may be spotted while the eagle is perched. The victim is caught after a brief aerial sprint and a swift pounce. Sometimes a pair of eagles may hunt co-operatively, one flushing the quarry while the second moves in behind to effect the kill. Flying birds can also be caught, the eagle nimbly snatching its victim in mid-air or else inflicting sufficient shock or injury to bring it to the ground. By this technique birds as large as geese, swans and capercaillie may be brought down.

The eagle's normal killing technique is to crush small prey in its strong talons. The claw on the hind toe is longer and more curved, piercing the body to inflict the *coup de grâce*. Larger mammals present more of a problem but since predators such as eagles cannot afford to be incapacitated, even for a short time, they will not normally risk tackling large or dangerous prey. Juvenile eagles, however, are less experienced and several have been known to strike full-grown deer, and once even a cow, only to be carried on the backs of the panic-stricken beasts until able to extricate their talons. Such incidents are rare but may have given rise to a common folk belief in the Scottish Highlands that the eagle blinds the animal with its wings while deliberately panicking it over a cliff.

This raises the question of just how much an eagle can lift. Normally large prey is dismembered on the spot and transported back to the nest in two or more portions. The evidence would suggest that an eagle is struggling to lift the equivalent of its own body weight (5 to 7 kg: 11 to 15 pounds) and even then may succeed only with the aid of favourable winds or gradient.

Estimates of an eagle's daily food requirements vary according to how active the bird is, the season and climatic conditions. Eagles in captivity demand less food than wild birds. Studies have indicated that captive, but exercised, adult golden eagles consumed between 260 and 300 grams (9 to 10½ ounces) per day (depending on sex) and this decreased by about 12 per cent in warm weather. This was equivalent to about 5 to 7 per cent of the body weight of the bird. There was also some evidence that the eagles needed to increase their food intake while moulting.

In the wild eagles need to kill a slight excess to allow for wastage — bones, feathers or fur which cannot be digested. Leslie Brown has estimated this to be about 20 to 30 per cent of each live kill. Juggling with figures, he went on to suggest that an average eagle home range would have to provide some 250 kg (595 pounds) of prey a year. This would normally comprise 127 kg (280 pounds) of mammal prey (equivalent to seventy mountain hares), 72 kg (159 pounds) of birds (about 126 grouse) and some 50 kg (110 pounds) of carrion.

EAGLES AND LAMBS

Eagles have long been blamed for killing lambs. Lambs do feature in the diet of a few pairs in the west Highlands, but the taking of a *live* lamb is rare. In some areas sheep carrion is an important food resource, but this is usually where live prey such as hares and grouse is scarce. Dead sheep can be important in the winter months especially. There is no scarcity of carrion at this time of year and in a 2 mile (3 km) stretch of Lewis moorland in the Outer Hebrides Jim Lockie and David Stephen encountered no less than 28 dead sheep. This reflected the poor quality of the ground, reinforced in many instances by poor management through overstocking, bad burning practice and poor husbandry.

If lambs are taken by eagles at all, most are found already dead — again a reflection of the poor grazing quality. About one-quarter of all lambs born in the west Highlands do not survive beyond a week or two. In a sample of 254 carcases autopsied in Argyll, David Houston found that 27 per cent had been stillborn, 57 per cent had died before they could walk, 9 per cent were diseased and 5 per cent had died accidentally. Amongst those for which no cause of death was immediately apparent, nearly half were starving. Others had reduced fat levels and only 7 per cent seemed healthy. Thus during lambing time there can be no shortage of carrion for eagles.

On rare occasions eagles may lift live lambs, although what proportion of these are in poor health is usually difficult to determine. The sporadic cases of lamb killing by eagles may often be prompted by a shortage of other food — an outbreak of myxomatosis amongst the local rabbits, or a loss of hunting range by too much afforestation.

To a crofter with a limited sheep stock, however, any loss of lambs to eagles can represent a significant financial burden. A system of cash compensation for reported eagle-killed lambs is not to be recommended. This merely encourages additional losses to be blamed on eagles in the hope of claiming more money. Hill farmers already attract sheep subsidies so perhaps those that keep sheep in golden eagle territory should be given a little extra in lieu of possible eagle losses. But shepherds should at the same time be encouraged to improve their husbandry, as this would bring much more significant reductions in mortality. It should also be remembered that eagles prey upon other species such as hooded crows, ravens, gulls, rabbits, even fox cubs, all of which may harm the farmer's livelihood.

Breeding cycle

COURTSHIP

The pair take advantage of any fine windy days in winter, gliding and soaring together for long periods, often at considerable height. Neighbouring pairs may overlap in home ranges but each usually maintains an exclusive 'core area' and rarely do they interact. Intruders tend to be immatures or subadults. An approach by the established pair may be a sufficient deterrent but sometimes purposeful stoops and dives are called for. Actual

11 (left). *A golden eagle eyrie. This is a cliff ledge but eagles will also nest in trees.*

12 (right). *A golden eagle nest with two nearly white eggs. Clutches of three are less common, as are single-egg clutches.*

13. *A one-week-old chick. Its tiny sibling, hatched out several days previously, has probably already died and has disappeared.*

14. *Adult golden eagle standing on its eyrie in front of its three-week-old chick.*

15. *Adult golden eagle bringing a fresh spray of rowan leaves to the eyrie; the three-week-old eaglet lies asleep.*

fights are rare.

Courtship between the pair may progress from 'mutual soaring' into a beautiful undulating flight display called 'sky-dancing'. One bird, usually the male, will dive on the other with half-closed wings. It needs only to open its wings fractionally and flap a few times to gain sufficient height to repeat the manoeuvre. Occasionally the female may roll over to present talons to the male as he passes. Rarely, if ever, do golden eagles grapple talons, as do sea eagles and some other raptors, although sometimes an exuberant juvenile may seem to attempt this to snatch food from its parent. Typically a sky-dance consists of a dozen stoops, the display fulfilling a territorial function as well as a courtship one.

Courtship may take place as early as January but is most frequent in March just before egg-laying. The act of copulation usually takes place on the ground, rarely at the nest, and may follow a bout of high-soaring or sky-dancing. The female solicits by leaning forwards; the male approaches with his wings held high, flapping to maintain balance as he covers her. After several seconds he dismounts.

HOME RANGE AND NESTS

The home range of an eagle may vary from 25 to 75 sq km (10 to 30 square miles) depending upon the abundance of prey. Outside Britain, in Switzerland or the United States for example, a pair may hold 180 sq km (70 square miles), although only a proportion of any territory may be regularly utilised.

Typically each home range contains two or three eyrie sites. Some pairs may have as many as a dozen but usually only one or two are favoured. These nests may be only a few metres apart or, in large ranges, several kilometres. Eyries are known to have been in use for decades, sometimes even centuries. Some pairs choose only cliff ledges, others nest only in trees, while a few have eyries in both. Nest building may begin as early as November, though it usually becomes intense in early spring. Both sexes collect sticks and occasionally unusual items may be incorporated into the nest — stags' antlers, a shepherd's crook, even coils of wire or binder twine. The nest cup is lined with dried grass, bracken or woodrush. Newly constructed nests are often quite small, barely 200 mm (8 inches) high and 1 metre (3 feet) across. Added to in subsequent years, old nests may become huge, nearly 5 metres (16 feet) in height and weighing over a tonne. In winter gales, with a heavy covering of snow, the nest, or even the tree, may collapse.

A study in Sweden showed that golden eagles selected the oldest trees, nearly always Scots pine. These provided the best foundations for a nest, when placed on the thickest and strongest boughs, usually near the top of the tree. On younger pines the nest was often placed on deformed or twisted branches, or on the dense growths known as 'witches' brooms'. Cliff nests often enjoy the additional support of a small bush or sapling in front, while an overhang of rock may give cover and shade. Fortunately few rock nests are easily accessible to humans.

EGGS AND INCUBATION

In Scotland egg-laying commences around mid March, sometimes as early as the first week. Around the Mediterranean eggs are laid as early as the end of January while in northern Europe they may not appear until late April or early May. Some late clutches may be the result of repeat layings but such instances are rare in golden eagles. A second egg is normally laid two to five days after the first. Three-egg clutches are less common and only two four-egg clutches seem to have been recorded. Museum clutches give a mean of 1.9 eggs, similar to figures quoted by Seton Gordon, who noted 18 per cent of clutches to contain only one egg and 10 per cent three eggs. The egg of a golden eagle is a rounded oval in shape and dull white in colour. Some bear red-brown spots, blotches or freckles. Usually one of the eagle's eggs is more blotched than the other, and the first egg tends to be slightly larger. A sample of one hundred Scottish eggs varied from 70 to 89 mm (2¾ to 3½ inches) in length, and 51 to 66 mm (2 to 2½ inches) in breadth (average 75 by 59 mm; 3 by 2⅜ inches). Weighing around

16. *A golden eagle incubating and showing its golden neck plumes and the beautiful reticulate pattern on its back and wings.*

17. *An adult golden eagle standing on the eyrie which contains two tiny eaglets (one is asleep in front of the other).*

18. *A two-week-old golden eagle chick with an unhatched egg (by now stained brown with wet peat, etcetera).*

19. *A three-week-old eaglet, still covered with white down and its crop bulging with food.*

20. *A three-week-old eaglet lying in its eyrie on the Isle of Rum and surrounded by prey remains of Manx shearwaters.*

21. *An eaglet five to six weeks old with its body feathers now well developed through the white down. The head feathers are amongst the last to come through.*

22. *This beautifully marked female eagle is feeding its two-week-old eaglet.*

140 grams (5 ounces), the egg is small for the size of the bird, equivalent to about 3 per cent of the female's body weight.

Incubation commences as soon as the first egg is laid. Pairs are very prone to desert at this time if disturbed. The bulk of brooding is undertaken by the female, and it is she who always sits overnight. Some males may strive to do an equal share of the duties, which allows the female to do a little hunting for herself. Lea MacNally knew of one male which continued to incubate the egg for several days after his mate had been killed. The incubation lasts 42 to 45 days.

NESTLING PERIOD

Feeble calls may be heard from an egg the day before it hatches. The newly emerged chick weighs about 105 grams (3¾ ounces) and is covered in white down. Its eyes are barely open and it can hardly lift its head. It is brooded constantly and, when awake, it keeps up a shrill peeping noise in a persistent demand for food.

Growth is rapid so that by the time the second chick hatches three or four days later the first weighs two and a half times as much. The parents still respond to the vigorous begging of the first-born, and only when it is satisfied does the second get a share. In one feeding bout the first chick was recorded receiving 72 morsels while the second got only two! A third chick is even more disadvantaged.

SIBLING RIVALRY

A reduction in brood size is common amongst many birds of prey. Some aggression between siblings clearly occurs. Seton Gordon termed this 'the Cain and

18

Abel battle'. Sometimes Cain pursues his little rival around the nest, pecking vigorously at his head or back, even pulling him about. The parents do nothing to intervene and eventually Abel succumbs to the ill treatment, from starvation or even because he was thrown from the nest.

Paradoxically such fierce sibling rivalry does have survival value. If food is in short supply, the younger chick (or chicks) quickly starve. The brood is thus reduced to a size that the parents can adequately feed. Attacks on the weaker chick merely hasten its demise, so that the health of the older is not compromised by having to share limited resources with a doomed sibling. The presence of an extra chick or two is merely an assurance in case food turns out to be more abundant. In such an instance all or both may be reared to fledging.

If the younger chick survives its first two or three weeks, the level of abuse is reduced and its chances are good. By this time the eaglets are sprouting feathers and can be left unattended for longer periods. They begin to tear up more and more food for themselves.

FLEDGING

Although the eaglet always strives to defecate well clear of the nest rim, the structure eventually becomes flattened and fouled with prey remains. Larger bones and carcases are usually removed by the adults. When the eaglet nears maturity it begins vigorous wing exercises. In the eleventh or twelfth week it finally takes wing. At first the youngster is reluctant to venture far because the adults continue to bring prey to the vicinity of the nest. It may be two months before it equals its parents in flying ability, and it then makes its first attempts at killing prey for itself. After three months it is more or less independent.

23. *An unusual portrait of both male and female golden eagles on the nest together. The female looks on while the male feeds some morsels of food to the eaglet.*

24 (left). *Twin eaglets almost fledged from a tree eyrie in the north-east Highlands. Usually older pine trees are favoured.*

25 (right). *Golden eagles are seldom used in falconry and require special licences. This bird was badly contaminated with oil spat at it by the fulmars it was catching. Although now cleaned, the old feathers are badly worn, contrasting with the new dark ones being moulted in.*

26. *Eagles are suffering extensive loss of hunting range because of blanket commercial forestry. This photograph was taken in Glen Spean near Fort William.*

Ringing recoveries show that few Scottish juveniles travel far afield — usually about 50 km (30 miles), with a maximum of 160 km (100 miles). On the continent, however, recoveries may occur as much as 2000 km (1250 miles) away. In northern Europe some adults may move south for the winter, whereas in Scotland they remain on territory throughout the year.

LONGEVITY AND MORTALITY

Although three-quarters of all young eagles may never reach maturity, those that do have the prospect of a relatively long life. In Switzerland the life expectancy is about twenty years. The oldest known ringed bird (from France) was 25 years 8 months old. In captivity golden eagles might be expected to live longer still and there are reliable records of some living to be nearly fifty. Seton Gordon was inclined to accept one record of a golden eagle being 95 but this seems unlikely.

Pairs generally remain faithful for life although cases are known of one female being ousted by another. In areas where persecution is rife young eagles may gain an opportunity to mate with an adult; rarely do such pairs produce eggs, however. Golden eagles probably do not become sexually mature until at least four years of age, but this is based only upon plumage characteristics rather than marked birds of known age.

On the Isle of Rum two golden eagles have been found which were apparently killed by red deer. It is thought that the birds were so gorged on the carcases of deer calves that they were unable to escape from the irate hinds returning to suckle their offspring. Both eagles had been trampled into the ground. There are also stories of golden eagles dying from wounds received when tackling full-grown wildcats or foxes. One or two golden eagles on the west coast of Scotland have been found with their plumage matted in the fishy oil spat out by their fulmar prey. Other eagles have been found dead after colliding with overhead power cables, or even aeroplanes. But such incidents are rare. Young eagles commonly die in their first year or two of life, often from starvation before they have perfected their hunting skills. By

27. *A hungry juvenile golden eagle standing on a crag having recently taken to the wing for the first time.*

far the most important cause of death is undoubtedly man. Despite legal protection, shooting, trapping and poisoning still take place.

Population dynamics

NESTING DENSITY

Watching a lone eagle in the rugged landscape of the Scottish Highlands, it is not hard to imagine that this creature is the master of all it surveys. In reality the golden eagle is, like all other life on earth, the product, even the servant, of its environment. So long as there is an adequate food supply, a safe nesting

21

place and freedom from the destructive influence of people, eagles will thrive. Except in flat and treeless country there is rarely a shortage of nesting sites. In some areas, most notably the eastern Highlands, numbers are depressed by human interference and the illegal use of poisons.

As a general rule eagle numbers are set by the amount of food available to them. Parts of the west of Scotland are remarkable in that they support some of the highest densities of golden eagles in Europe, and perhaps the world. Here territories can be as small as 25 sq km (10 square miles) leading to a density of around 40 pairs per 1000 sq km (386 square miles). The comparable figures for the eastern Highlands, free from persecution, is some 15 pairs per 1000 sq km. In Scandinavia the natural density is lower still at 8 to 10 pairs per 1000 sq km, and in parts of Italy down to 4 pairs per 1000 sq km.

These differences are linked to variations in the amount of food, and more precisely to how much food there is in winter. Eagles feed substantially on carrion at this time. Indeed, in western Scotland it is the abundance of sheep and red deer carrion which is largely responsible for the high densities. In eastern Scotland there is much deer but little sheep carrion, while in the low-density European populations carrion is either absent or else available only in direct competition with other large scavengers such as vultures and carnivorous mammals.

BREEDING PERFORMANCE

Some fluctuations in eagle breeding success can be caused by weather. It seems that prolonged cold and wet weather in March and April can cause pairs to fail early or not to breed at all. Typically across Europe, golden eagles rear around 0.5 chicks per pair per year. In Scotland the average is similar, although there is considerable variation across the country. Over much of the west-central Highlands the figure is as low as 0.3, whilst in the east Highlands (in the absence of persecution) an average of 0.7 chicks per pair per year is normal, and broods of two are quite

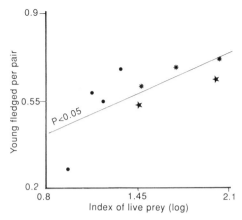

28. *Relationship between golden eagle breeding success and the amount of live prey available. The success data were derived from about fifteen pairs over five years for each area (1981-5). The food index (plotted on a log scale) was collected 1982-5. Data recalculated from Watson, Langslow and Rae, 1987.*

common. These differences are mainly attributable to the abundance of food in summer, when the young are being reared. Once the eagles have negotiated the vagaries of weather in spring, and assuming they are free from human persecution, their prospect of successful nesting is largely determined by the numbers of three or four key prey species.

In the east Highlands breeding success is high where, and whenever, red grouse and mountain hare numbers are high. In south Argyll and the Inner Hebrides there are still locally plentiful rabbit populations; when their numbers are high the eagles breed well. In the north-west Highlands and on some of the islands seabirds, notably fulmars, are important also. In these areas typical eagle production figures are close to the national average. Where rabbits and seabirds are scarce, as they are over much of the west-central Highlands, breeding success can be very low indeed, less than 0.2 chicks per pair in some years. Most eagles do not take heavy items of carrion, such as pieces of dead sheep or deer, to their nests. This type of food is short in essential nutrients, such as calcium, which growing eaglets require. Eagles do take smaller items of carrion to the nest but dead lambs, for instance, are available only for a short period during the spring and could not alone sustain a breeding attempt.

Another clear example of the link between breeding success and food supply comes from America. In the western United States golden eagles depend very largely on black-tailed jack-rabbits, and breeding success has been shown to follow closely the cycles of abundance of this prey species every eight or ten years. Here the breeding success of eagles may drop as low as 0.1 chick per pair in poor years but can peak at 1.5, with many nests containing two chicks in good years.

Once they are adult, golden eagles might be expected to have a breeding life of about twenty years. With an average production of 0.5 chicks fledged per pair per year, and an estimated 75 per cent juvenile mortality rate, a pair living for twenty years should produce enough young to replace themselves. However, this equation is finely balanced and it would not take much of a drop, either in life expectancy or in breeding performance, to precipitate a decline in eagle numbers.

THREATS AND THE FUTURE

The comparatively healthy state of Scottish golden eagles is no justification for complacency. Their value to mankind as crucial biological indicators of the health of our natural environment has been well demonstrated. During the 1960s peregrine falcon and sparrowhawk populations were severely reduced when breeding failures were brought about by the accumulative effects of organo-chlorine pesticides, with DDT the main culprit. Golden eagles were also implicated in this debate and poor breeding performance in parts of western Scotland in the mid 1960s was attributed to contamination from the sheep dip Dieldrin, ingested by eagles which fed on the carcases. More recently there has been concern over the levels of other man-made pollutants, polychlorinated biphenyls (PCBs), which have reached worrying levels in the sea, including the waters off western Scotland. In this area some golden eagles feed partly on seabirds, which are known to accumulate high levels of PCBs in their body tissues. Further research is needed to determine whether the eagles' breeding success may be affected.

The continued persecution of golden eagles in parts of eastern Scotland remains a tragic legacy of nineteenth-century thinking and arrogance. Although all predatory birds have been fully protected in Britain since the early 1950s, there remains an element in society who continue to flout the law. This is slowly changing, but continued vigilance is needed and it is imperative that anyone finding a dead eagle in suspicious circumstances should inform the conservation authorities immediately.

Since 1945, and increasingly since the 1960s, the biggest single change to the eagle's landscape has been the wholesale conversion of sheepwalk to plantation forestry. This has been most conspicuous in south-west Scotland and in the south-western Highlands. The consequence of extensive conifer plantations is to eliminate the eagle's food or the hunting potential of large tracts of land at low and middle altitudes. In Galloway the recovery of the golden eagle population since 1945 may now have been stalled by the massive afforestation of the uplands, and its breeding success has declined in those territories most severely affected by planting. In Argyll there is evidence that as many as 30 per cent of the eagle territories occupied around 1960 are no longer used, and the future of several others is bleak as the blanket of commercial forest spreads.

Britain still harbours one of the largest populations of golden eagles in Europe. It is the clear responsibility of everyone to ensure that we do not easily abandon this privilege.

Further reading

Brown, L. H., and Watson, A. 'The Golden Eagle in Relation to Its Food Supply', *Ibis*, 106 (1964), 78-100.

Dennis, R. H.; Ellis, P. M.; Broad, R. A.; and Langslow, D. R. 'The Status of the Golden Eagle in Britain', *British Birds*, 77 (1984), 592-602.

Gordon, S. *The Golden Eagle, King of Birds*. Collins, 1955.

Lockie, J. D.; Ratcliffe, D.; and Balharry, R. 'Breeding Success and Organo-chlorine Residues in Golden Eagles in West Scotland', *Journal of Applied Ecology*, 6 (1969), 381-9.

Lockie, J. D., and Stephen, D. 'Eagles, Lambs and Lamb Management in Lewis', *Journal of Animal Ecology*, 28 (1959), 43-50.

Love, J. A. *The Return of the Sea Eagle*. Cambridge University Press, 1983.

Love, J. A. *Eagles*. Whittet, 1989.

MacNally, L. *The Ways of an Eagle*. Collins, 1977.

Marquiss, M.; Ratcliffe, D. A.; and Roxburgh, R. 'The Numbers, Breeding Success and Diet of Golden Eagles in Southern Scotland in Relation to Changes in Land-use', *Biological Conservation*, 33 (1985), 1-17.

Newton, I. *Population Ecology of Raptors*. Poyser, 1979.

Sandeman, P. 'The Breeding Success of Golden Eagles in the Southern Grampians', *Scottish Naturalist*, 69 (1957), 148-52.

Tomkies, M. *Golden Eagle Years*. Heinemann, 1982.

Watson, A.; Payne, S.; and Rae, R. 'Golden Eagles *Aquila chrysaetos*: Land Use and Food in Northeast Scotland', *Ibis*, 131 (1989), 336-48.

Watson, J.; Langslow, D. R.; and Rae, S. R. *The Impact of Land-use Changes on Golden Eagles in the Scottish Highlands*. Nature Conservancy Council, Peterborough, 1987.

ACKNOWLEDGEMENTS

Photographs are acknowledged as follows: Eric and David Hosking (N. Rankin), 22, 23; Frank Lane Picture Agency (A. Christiansen), 3; L. MacNally, 8, 14, 15, 16, 17, 27. Photographs 7, 9, 10, 20, 21, 24, 25, 26 and the cover are by J. A. Love, and photographs 6, 11, 12, 13, 18 and 19 are by J. Watson. Figure 1 is by J. A. Love.